Jane Brocket's CLEVER CONCEPTS

Spotty, Stripy, Swirly

What are PATTERNS?

Millbrook Press • Minneapolis

Look at what you are wearing today. Do you see any patterns?

When something is repeated or set out in a special order, it creates a

PATTERN.

Patterns can be made with shapes, colors, or objects. Let's look around to see what patterns we can find.

If things are jumbled up, there is no pattern. But when they are put in lines and rows, patterns start to appear.

Some patterns are simple.

Others are more complicated. These stitched circles overlap and make many different patterns.

Look carefully, and you will find lots of patterns in nature. Patterns on plants help us to know what they are.

The repeating colors and shapes on this flower tell us it's a dahlia.

Geranium leaves all have the same shape and pattern of colors on them.

Patterns help us decorate. The candies on this cake make patterns with curls, swirls, and lots of spots and dots.

Shapes and colors make cheerful patterns on blankets and quilts.

Patterns help us predict and plan. They make it easy for us to know what comes next.

The gardener who planted these swirly lettuces used different patterns. How many do you see?

13

Stripes make good patterns. They can go across, down, or up and down in a spiky zigzag.

Look at the patterns left behind after a day at the beach.

Someone has set out pebbles in circles, lines, and groups.

Some are in groups of two, and some are in groups of three. Some are set out by color, and others are set out by size.

Fabric squares are sewn together in a pattern to make a quilt. Do you see more patterns in the fabrics?

Square tiles make patterns too. Look at how the tiles repeat patterns and colors over and over to make a bigger pattern.

19

When you play with objects, you can discover all sorts of patterns. Look how many patterns can be made with just one thing.

Cookies can be arranged
by colors or numbers.

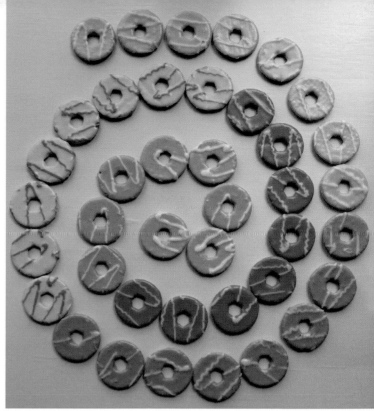

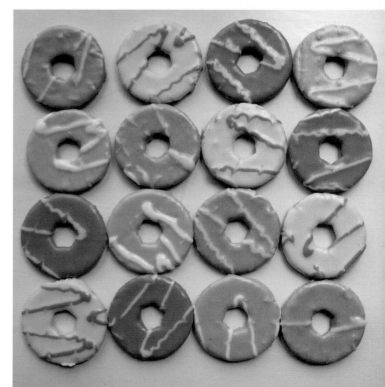

In plain rows and lines or
in fancy, colorful swirls.

Buildings often have patterns on them. A skyscraper is made of triangles that fit together in a pattern. Another building has a neat pattern of round windows.

This old wall has lots of patterns. Can you spot them all?

Don't forget to look inside buildings too. Look up and down and all around at ceilings, walls, stairs, and floors. You might find lots of interesting patterns . . . and some might make you feel very dizzy!

It's easy to make patterns with spots. Spots can be lined up in rows. They can be close together or spread out.

When spots are set out in a regular pattern, they are called polka dots.

27

Patterns appear on sunny days, when the sun makes shadows all around.

You can make patterns appear too.

Brightly colored flowers are fun
to arrange in rows and groups.

The world is full of interesting patterns. Dotty, spotty, curly, swirly. Straight and bendy, neat and wavy, crisscross and curvy. **Do you have a favorite PATTERN?**

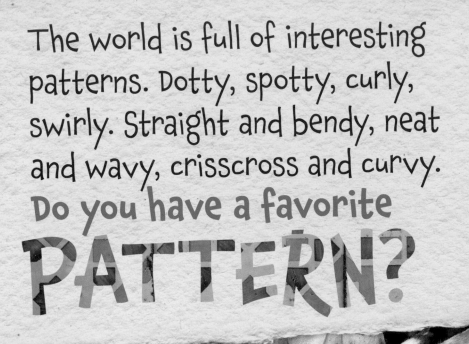

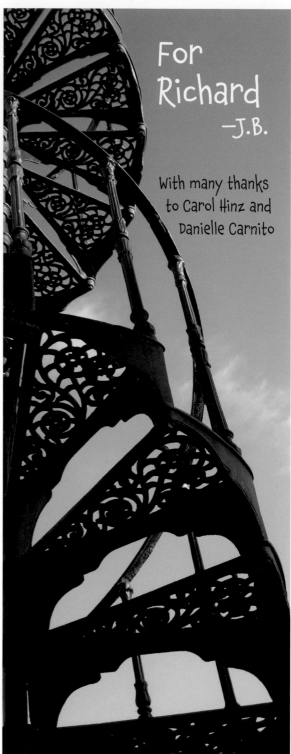

For
Richard
—J.B.

With many thanks
to Carol Hinz and
Danielle Carnito

Text and photographs copyright © 2012 by Jane Brocket

Millbrook Press
A division of Lerner Publishing Group, Inc.
241 First Avenue North
Minneapolis, MN 55401 U.S.A.

Website address: www.lernerbooks.com

Main body text set in Chaloops Regular 24/32.
Typeface provided by Chank.

Library of Congress Cataloging-in-Publication Data

Brocket, Jane.
    Spotty, stripy, swirly : what are patterns? / written and photographed
  by Jane Brocket.
       p.   cm. — (Jane brocket's clever concepts)
    ISBN 978-0-7613-4613-5 (lib. bdg. : alk. paper)
    1. Pattern perception—Juvenile literature. I. Title.
  BF294.B76 2012
  152.14'23—dc23   2011022179

Manufactured in the United States of America
1 — DP — 12/31/11